THE THEATRE MACHINE 2

A Resource Manual for Teaching Acting

By

Albert T. Viola

Pioneer
DRAMA SERVICE

ACKNOWLEDGEMENT

I want to thank my wife Helen Pallas-Viola for her support and help during the writing of this text.
I also want to thank Jennifer Malloy, my student assistant, and the countless students
who participated in the development of these lessons and exercises.

-ATV

Published in 1996 by Pioneer Drama Service, Inc.
P.O. Box 4267
Englewood, CO 80155-4267

TABLE OF CONTENTS

One Person Improvisation

Two Person Obscure Dialogue Scene

Solo Intentions

CHOICES, GOALS
AND THE SEVEN Ws

LESSON ONE

What Is The Scene About?

The First W

OBJECTIVE: To establish and maintain the reality of a scene in a specific place and situation.

ACTIVITY: Two students engage in an improvisation. The necessary element of the improvisation is the concept of the first W, the place (What is the scene about?). Select or have two students volunteer to do an improvisation between employer and an employee candidate.

The scene is about a student interviewing for a job because the student wants to start earning money in order to buy (have the student select one of the following):

1. ...a car

2. ...a stereo

3. ...roller blades

4. ...a new T.V. and video games

5. ...plane tickets for a trip

6. ...a season ticket to a favorite sports team's games

7. ...some new clothes that are in fashion that Mom and Dad won't buy

8. ...tickets to entertainment events, rock concerts, etc.

9. ...a new computer with all the software

10. ...refreshments to throw a big party

The job he is applying for is (select one of the following):

1. ...babysitter

2. ...newspaper delivery person

3. ...clerk in a cut rate drug store

4. ...McDonald's cashier

5. ...busperson at a restaurant

6. ...hospital aid

7. ...library assistant

8. ...dog groomer

9. ...pet sitter

10. ...amusement park attendant

COACHING TIPS: Ask the class what they thought of the improvisation and if it was clear to them. Was the scene believable? Make sure the students address you and not the students doing the improvisation. You then should evaluate the scene as you see it, pointing out the good points as well as those that need attention.

LESSON TWO

Who Am I? Part I

The Second W

OBJECTIVE: To define the physiognomy and psychological traits of a character.

ACTIVITY: Each student will use specific physical activities to represent an individual of a certain age as she goes to a bench and waits for a bus. Each student must answer the list of character traits before starting a scene or an improvisation. The instructor should give the student the age on a slip of paper and the class should guess what age is being portrayed or represented.

EXAMPLE: A person of eighty-five years of age might walk to the bus stop very slowly with a cane or a walker. She may be bent over because she is weak and frail, though she may try to act more vigorous than she is. She might take out her glasses and clean them so that she can read the bus stop sign. She may check her watch, then take out a pill box and take a pill.

Character Traits:

1. Age

2. Height

3. Weight

4. Hair

5. Eyes

6. Overall health

7. Religion

8. Morals

9. Family background

10. Self-esteem

Go to a bench and wait for a bus as if you were. . .

1.. . . three years old.

2.. . . six years old.

3.. . . twelve years old.

4.. . . sixteen years old.

5.. . . twenty-one years old.

6.. . . fifty years old.

7.. . . sixty-five years old.

8.. . . ninety years old.

COACHING TIP: Go over the ten character traits and ask the students questions. Did the class guess the age? What could else have been done to depict the proper age? Was it too young? Too old?

LESSON THREE

Who Am I? Part II

The Second W

OBJECTIVE: To strengthen the imagination in portraying a character while developing taste and selectivity.

ACTIVITY: Each student will use specific physical activities in pantomime to represent a certain professional. Each pantomime should have a beginning, a middle and an end.

EXAMPLE: A short-order cook opens up his shop, puts on his apron and hat and prepares his grill (the beginning). He gets the ingredients he needs for his various meal orders. Once he is set, he starts taking orders that are hung on clips above him (the middle). He then proceeds to prepare his first meal of the day. He sets the plate up and rings a bell, informing the waiter or waitress that the meal is ready (the end).

Possible Professions:

1. Accountant	11. Architect
2. Computer operator	12. Artist
3. Graphic designer	13. Mechanic
4. Housekeeper	14. Banker
5. Printer	15. Model
6. Locksmith	16. Photographer
7. Tow truck operator	17. Hairstylist
8. Dry cleaning operator	18. Manicurist
9. Archery instructor	19. Rug cleaner
10. Land surveyor	20. Carpet layer

COACHING TIP: Did the improvisation have a beginning, a middle and an end? Did the student's physical activities depict the profession? Was it too general? If so, what could he have included to make it more specific? Did the student believe who he was? Is the concept "Who am I?" understood by the student?

LESSON FOUR

Who Am I? Part III

The Second W

OBJECTIVE: To strengthen the imagination in portraying a character while developing taste and selectivity and working with props.

ACTIVITY: Each student will incorporate an actual prop into a scene using specific physical activities to represent a profession. Each scene should have a beginning, a middle and an end.

EXAMPLE: Prop: A clipboard. A person pantomimes pushing a cart down the lane of a supermarket and stops at a particular shelf. She takes inventory of the items on the shelf. After she counts the items, she enters the number on the paper on the clipboard. She then opens a box on the cart, takes out some cans and refills the shelf. She enters the number of cans she has placed on the shelf on the clipboard. She may do the same thing with other items. After she finishes, she leaves with her cart.

Possible Props:

1. Ball	11. Spatula
2. Frying pan	12. Eye glasses
3. Clipboard	13. Vacuum cleaner
4. Stopwatch	14. Book
5. Stethoscope	15. Tool
6. Briefcase	16. Rope
7. Whistle	17. Hammer
8. Tire gauge	18. Plunger
9. Magnifying glass	19. Telephone
10. Paintbrush	20. Radio

COACHING TIP: Did the scene have a beginning, a middle and an end? Did the student's physical activities depict the profession? Was it too general? If so, what could she have done to make it more specific? Was the prop used effectively? Did the student believe who she was? Is the concept "Who am I?" understood by the student?

LESSON FIVE

Who Am I? Part IV

The Second W

OBJECTIVE: To strengthen the imagination in developing a character while using specific physical activities in pantomime.

ACTIVITY: Ask each student to incorporate specific physical activities in a pantomime that conveys the place where he works.

1. A priest in a church

2. A lifeguard at a pool

3. A ticket-taker at a movie theater

4. A policeman in a jail

5. A guard in a museum

6. A manager at a health food store

7. A clerk at a record store

8. A teacher in a classroom

9. A dentist in an office

10. A farmer in a barn

11. A teacher in a gym

12. A scientist in a laboratory

13. A worker in a lumber yard

14. A worker in a fast food restaurant

15. A worker in an ice cream shop

16. A worker in a zoo

17. A nurse in a hospital

18. A cook in a pizza parlor

19. A baker in a bakery shop

20. A clerk in a pet store

COACHING TIPS: Was the pantomime simple and direct? Could the audience tell where the student worked?

LESSON SIX

Where Am I? Part I

The Third W

OBJECTIVE: To strengthen the imagination and ability to identify a place through the five senses: taste, hearing, touch, smell and sight.

ACTIVITY: Each student pantomimes a simple physical activity and brings to life the atmosphere of the location she has chosen by using one or more of the five senses.

1. A desert	11. A school
2. His/her room	12. A place of work
3. A dance hall	13. A hospital
4. An athletic event	14. A supermarket
5. A cultural event	15. A circus
6. A movie house	16. A cemetery
7. A church/synagogue	17. A mall
8. A museum	18. A pizza restaurant
9. An airplane	19. A skating rink
10. A train	20. A library

COACHING TIPS: Did the student use one or more of the five senses? Ask the student to describe the place. If it was not clear, you might ask, "What are you smelling?" and "What sounds are you hearing?" Was the actor merely indicating or did the actor believe she was there?

LESSON SEVEN

Where Am I? Part II

The Third W

OBJECTIVE: To strengthen the imagination and selectivity in establishing the setting for a scene.

ACTIVITY: Have each student select one of the places listed below and incorporate specific physical activities in a pantomime to convey that he is in that location. The student should plan a beginning, a middle and an end.

Possible Places:

1. In a kitchen	11. In a spaceship
2. In a gas station	12. In a video store
3. In a canoe	13. In a school
4. In a ski shop	14. In a cave
5. On a roof	15. In a restaurant
6. In a barbershop	16. On a beach
7. In a hair salon	17. In a mall
8. In a church	18. At a formal dinner table
9. On a train	19. In a shoe store
10. In a library	20. In a stereo shop

COACHING TIPS: Did the student incorporate specific physical activities to determine where he was? Was there a beginning, a middle and an end?

LESSON EIGHT

What Am I Doing? Part I

The Fourth W

OBJECTIVE: To establish and maintain the reality of a simple physical activity.

ACTIVITY: The following physical activities must be done in pantomime and without props:

1. Wash your dog
2. Wash the car
3. Mow the lawn
4. Build a fire
5. Make a pizza
6. Thread a needle
7. Screw in a light bulb
8. Open a drink and pour it in a cup
9. Peel an orange
10. Sharpen a pencil
11. Put on a sports outfit
12. Eat a plate of spaghetti
13. Polish your shoes
14. Put some new laces on your sneakers
15. Build a sand castle
16. Wrap a present
17. Write a letter
18. Wash dishes
19. Set the table
20. Make a sandwich

COACHING TIPS: Did the student present detailed, well-executed movements? Was she convincing? Was there a beginning, a middle and an end? Was it believable?

LESSON NINE

What Am I Doing? Part II

The Fourth W

OBJECTIVE: To think logically about a scene to create realistic physical activities.

ACTIVITY: Have each student select a set of physical activities listed below and perform them.

1.

        A. Put on pajamas

        B. Brush your teeth

        C. Wash your face

        D. Set your alarm clock

        E. Turn down your bed and get in it

What are you literally doing? PREPARING TO GO TO BED.

2.

        A. Take out your suitcase from the closet

        B. Select various clothes to place in the suitcase

        C. Select shoes, socks and undergarments and place in suitcase along with the clothes

        D. Select toilet items and place in suitcase

        E. Close suitcase

What are you literally doing? PREPARING TO TAKE A TRIP.

3.

        A. Put up a Christmas tree in the front room

        B. Take out a box of Christmas decorations from the closet

        C. Take out the box of lights, tinsel and colored decorations

        D. Place the decorations carefully on the tree

What are you literally doing? DECORATING A CHRISTMAS TREE.

4.

        A. Go to the closet and select some clothes

        B. Select a dress/pants and shirt/blouse

        C. Select shoes and socks

D. Comb hair and/or put on make-up

What are you literally doing? PREPARING TO GET DRESSED.

COACHING TIPS: Was the student specific with each physical activity? Was the student truthful?

LESSON TEN

What Do I Want? Why Do I Want It? Part I

The Fifth and Sixth Ws

OBJECTIVE: To think logically about a scene while knowing what the character is doing and why he is doing it. This is the execution of a Simple Physical Action.

ACTIVITY: A student engages in a pantomime repeating the previously executed Physical Activities in Lesson Nine, but this time with the addition of an Action/Task. When you know WHY the character is performing the physical activity, you are then performing a Simple Physical Action (the process of performing a physical activity and knowing the reason why). The combination of a Physical Activity and an Action/Task results in a Simple Physical Action. Knowing the reason WHY you are doing WHAT you are doing will give you the answer of HOW to do it.

As the student executes the five physical activities for PREPARING TO GO TO BED, he should incorporate one of the following reasons:

A. You have been sent to bed as a punishment for something you did. (Let the student determine what he has done.)

B. You must go to bed early because in the morning you are going to Europe for three months.

C. You are going to bed because you are sick but your mother wants you to brush your teeth and wash your face first.

D. You are going to bed to watch your favorite television show that is about to come on.

E. You are going to bed because in the morning you are moving to another state.

F. You must get some sleep because of a big test in the morning.

G. You have fallen asleep downstairs because it is late and now must go to bed.

H. You are going to bed because you have been hiking all day and you are out of shape and exhausted.

I. You are going to bed because you have a lights-out curfew and you have been in trouble before.

J. You want to go to bed but you promised to call a friend before it gets too late.

Suggested tools you might want to consider to help you with the execution of your physical activity:

1. with anger   6. with happiness/joy

2. with determination   7. with anticipation

3. with excitement   8. with boldness

4. with exhaustion   9. with desperation

5. with lethargy   10. with hope

COACHING TIPS: The student should do the physical activities with familiarity. It is suggested that the student try and recreate his own room and bathroom. Each student should be very specific about the activities. Make sure the student completes all five steps (physical activities) such as putting on pajamas, brushing teeth, washing face, setting alarm clock, turning down bed. Did the student make the physical activities clean and specific? If not, have the student do each separately. For example, with brushing teeth: pickup the tube of toothpaste, open it, pick up the tooth-brush and squeeze the toothpaste on it, brush teeth, fill cup with water and rinse mouth, place cup back, clean the toothbrush, put the cap back on the tube of toothpaste. The student may have his own way of brushing, so let him do it his way. However, make sure he has not forgotten anything. Once this is clear and specific he can now concentrate on the "tools" and psychological motivation of the scene. Familiarity on stage results in truthfulness and relaxation. If the actor believes what he is doing, so will the audience!

LESSON ELEVEN

What Do I Want? Why Do I Want It? Part II

The Fifth and Sixth Ws

OBJECTIVE: To think logically about a scene while knowing what the character is doing and why she is doing it. This is the execution of a Simple Physical Action.

ACTIVITY: A student engages in a pantomime repeating the previously executed Physical Activities in Lesson Nine, but this time with the addition of an Action/Task. When you know WHY the character is performing the physical activity, you are then performing a Simple Physical Action (the process of performing a physical activity and knowing the reason why). The combination of a Physical Activity and an Action/Task results in a Simple Physical Action. Knowing the reason WHY you are doing WHAT you are doing will tell you HOW to do it.

PREPARING TO TAKE A TRIP

    A. You are going to spend the summer with a relative that you are not fond of and who does not understand you or your orange hair.

    B. You are spending the weekend with your best friend whose parents let you do anything you want.

    C. You are going on a camping trip where you will sleep on the hard ground and use rocks for pillows. This is not your thing!

    D. You have been chosen to go around the world on a sailboat with an international group of students.

    E. You are going for a mandatory summer vacation with the family. You would much rather go to camp.

    F. You have been invited to spend the summer with your best friend, whose parents are explorers. You are going to the rain forest in Brazil.

    G. You are off to tennis camp and will be taught by top professionals.

    H. You will be attending a professional theater camp.

    I. You are going someplace you have never been before but the boy/girl you like most will be there.

Suggested "tools" you may want to consider to help you in your execution of the physical activity:

1. with reluctance	6. with disappointment
2. with anger	7. with apprehension
3. with joy	8. with nonchalance
4. with sadness	9. with happiness
5. with despondency	10. with determination

COACHING TIPS: The student should do the physical activities with familiarity. It is suggested that the student try and recreate her own room and bathroom. Each student should be very specific about the activities. Once this is clear and specific she can now concentrate on the "tools" and psychological motivation of the scene. Familiarity on stage results in truthfulness and relaxation. If the actor believes what she is doing, so will the audience.

LESSON TWELVE

What Do I Want? Why Do I Want It? Part III

The Fifth and Sixth Ws

OBJECTIVE: To think logically about a scene while knowing what the character is doing and why he is doing it. This is the execution of a Simple Physical Action.

ACTIVITY: A student engages in a pantomime repeating previously executed Physical Activities in Lesson Nine, but this time with the addition of an action/task.

PREPARING TO GET DRESSED

> A. You are going to a party.
>
> B. You have a date with a new boy/girlfriend.
>
> C. You have a blind date and you do not know what to expect.
>
> D. You are putting on a costume for a play you are in.
>
> E. You have a big exam that you did not study for.
>
> F. You are going to a concert by your favorite rock artist.
>
> G. You are going to your favorite sports event.
>
> H. You are going to a classical concert with your parents.
>
> I. You are going to church/synagogue.

Suggested "tools" you may want to consider in order to help you with the execution of the physical action:

1. with aprehension
2. with confidence
3. with excitement
4. with nonchalance
5. with indifference
6. with anger
7. with joy/happiness
8. with determination
9. with sadness
10. with ebullience

COACHING TIPS: Make sure the student completes all five steps (physical activities). Was the scene believable?

COACHING TIPS FOR TOOLS: After the student has mastered the "beats" for preparing to get dressed, have him repeat the scene with a "tool." For instance, if anger is the chosen tool, the actor might pull the drawers out of the dresser, grab socks and undergarments and throw them on the bed. Shirt and pants will be thrown on the bed with the hangers on. The selection process will be minimal. He will barely look in the mirror to check on his hair. The beat executed with controlled carelessness and great force will give the impression of "anger" or someone who is angry. However, to make it "real," the student must have a personal reason for why he is angry, creating a Simple Physical Action.

LESSON THIRTEEN

What Do I Want? Why Do I Want It? Part IV

The Fifth and Sixth Ws

OBJECTIVE: To think logically about a scene while knowing what the character is doing and why she is doing it. This is the execution of a Simple Physical Action.

ACTIVITY: A student is selected to perform one of the following Simple Physical Actions:

1. You are ironing some clothes because...

    A. ...you are going to a wedding.

    B. ...you are going to the funeral of a best friend.

    C. ...you are going on a first date.

    D. ...you are leaving for Europe and you're late and a cab is outside waiting.

    E. ...you are grounded and your mother has assigned you the extra task of ironing some family items.

2. You are writing a letter...

    A. ...to someone you love.

    B. ...to say goodbye forever to someone you love.

    C. ...to the mother of your best friend, who died.

    D. ...relating the funniest joke you ever heard.

3. You are packing for a trip...

    A. ...to visit a relative you do not get along with.

    B. ...you have just won a multi-million dollar lottery and are taking the family around the world.

    C. ...you have just been informed that there was a traffic accident in another town and a member of your family is hurt.

4. You are getting dressed because...

A. ...you are going to visit friends of your parents whom you do not know.

B. ...you are going to a new school and you do not know anybody there.

C. ...you are going to the mall with your best friend.

D. ...you are going to a birthday party given in your honor.

E. ...you are going out with a new boy/girlfriend.

F. ...you are going to a dance.

G. ...you are going to babysit two uncontrollable children.

COACHING TIPS: Make sure the student is specific, e.g. she knows the garment/garments she is ironing or packing. Ask her to describe each item. Was she specific while ironing? Have her iron or pack in her room at home in order to bring familiarity to the exercise. Was she believable? Did each student understand the concept of HOW to do a physical action once she knew WHY she was doing WHAT she was doing?

LESSON FOURTEEN

The Magnificent Seven, Part I

Putting It Together

or

The Six Ws Plus the Seventh W: What do I have to do to get what I want?

OBJECTIVE: To think logically and break down a scene by answering the questions of the Seven Ws, creating moment-to-moment reality and dealing with elements of conflict in an improvisational situation.

ACTIVITY: Two students engage in an improvisation. Have them agree on the answers to the Seven Ws and who is to play which role.

EXAMPLE: You have just been called into the principal's office because someone told the principal you took a tennis racket from a student's locker. You know who took it but you don't want to turn in your best friend.

First W:

    Q: What is the scene about?

    A: It is about you being accused of a crime you did not commit.

Second W:

    Q: Who am I?

    A: A high school student.

Third W:

    Q: Where am I?

    A: In the principal's office.

Fourth W:

    Q: What am I physically doing?

    A: Sitting in a chair feeling nervous and frightened. (Think about: What would I do in such a situation? What is going through my mind? What is my relationship with the principal?)

Fifth W:

Q: What do I want?

A: To prove my innocence.

Sixth W:

Q: Why do I want to prove my innocence?

A: Because I didn't do it and I could be expelled or suspended from school and my parents would be very disappointed in me.

Seventh W:

Q: What do I have to do to get what I want?

A. I must convince the principal it was not me but someone else, without telling him who it was.

SITUATIONS:

1. A teammate of yours has asked you to hurt one of the best players on the team you will be playing tomorrow in the championship game. It could mean the difference of glory for you, the team and the school. It is against your morals to do such a deed.

2. You have been away on vacation and have discovered that your best friend has been dating your boy/girlfriend. You confront your friend.

3. A friend asks you if she can stay over for the night. You agree. You discover that she only asked you because a boy is coming over to pick her up and she has asked you to lie to her parents.

4. You have friend over for the weekend while your parents are away. Your friend has invited several other people who in turn have invited others. The last count was around 120 people. You have been told by your parents that no one is to come into the house except your one invited friend. You must confront your friend.

5. You are playing your rival school. You have been asked by a fellow student, whose group you have been trying to be part of all year, to join them for a ride. You discover they are going to break the windows of the other school and steal the bell. You know this is wrong and do not want to participate but you do not want to jeopardize your invitation to join the group.

6. You are away at camp and sharing a room with another boy/girl. You auditioned for a movie you heard about that has nothing to do with the camp. You have been telling your roommate about everything and you are

waiting for a phone call from the producers because you are a finalist. The phone rings. The call is for your roommate. You discover that your roommate secretly auditioned because of the information you shared with him/her. Your roommate got the part. You confront your roommate.

7. You just broke up with your boy/girlfriend and you have been fixed up with a blind date who really likes you. You are very cautious about the relationship, yet you do not want to discourage the relationship from blossoming. You've arranged to meet your new friend for a soda to discuss your relationship.

8. You have been sent home from school for something you have done. You are confronted by your mother/father.

9. Some boy/girl has been following you and has an enormous crush on you. You are not interested in developing a relationship. You confront him/her. She/he won't take no for an answer.

10. You discover that a friend who slept over is drinking your parents' liquor. You confront him/her, and he/she promises to replace the consumed alcohol.

COACHING TIPS: Did the students break down the situations into the Seven Ws? Were the students serious and believable while performing?

LESSON FIFTEEN

The Magnificent Seven   Part II

Putting It Together

or

The Six Ws Plus the Seventh W: What do I have to do to get what I want?

OBJECTIVE: To think logically and specifically in performing an improvisation involving the elements of hot or cold by answering the questions of the Seven Ws.

ACTIVITY: Two students engage in an improvisation based on a given situation. The students make up the given circumstances that will clearly define the answers to the Seven Ws. The students must also create the atmosphere of hot or cold.

WORKING WITH COLD: Everyone gets cold differently. It depends on the degree of cold. With some people the ears become cold first, then the nose. With others it may be the toes or cheeks. You must ask yourself, "What gets cold first in my body?" And as it gets colder, how does the feeling spread? Then, when you are cold, how do you try to get warm? If your hands become cold first, you will most likely rub them together, blow heat from your mouth on them, etc. You may also go to a fire, rub your hands over it and maybe even turn so your backside can feel the heat. You may also find a blanket, gloves or anything that might give you warmth.

WORKING WITH HEAT: As with cold, everyone also gets hot differently. You may start to perspire on the forehead, under the nose or on the nape of your neck (particularly if you have long hair). Once you create the heat, you need to try and cool off. This is done by lifting your hair off the back of your neck, opening the collar of a shirt, using an object to fan yourself.

EXAMPLE: A daughter asks her mother if she can go to a concert. The mother says she cannot go because she received poor grades last quarter. The daughter disagrees and tries to convince her mother that she should go. Atmosphere: The furnace has gone out and there is no heat in the house. It is now 32 degrees and getting colder. The feeling of being cold should be incorporated in the improvisation.

First W:

Q: What is the scene about?

A: A mother and daughter having a disagreement.

Second W:

Q: Who am I?

A: The daughter who is popular in school but is having problems in a few classes.

Third W:

Q: Where am I?

A: In the kitchen.

Fourth W:

Q: What am I doing?

A: Helping my mother clear the supper table.

Fifth W:

Q: What do I want?

A: To convince my mother to let me go to the rock concert with my friends.

Sixth W:

Q: Why do I want it?

A: Because it would be fun and everyone is going. All my friends are assuming I'll be able to go, and it will be embarassing if I have to tell them I can't.

Seventh W:

Q: What do I have to do to get what I want?

A: I have to "convince" or "persuade" my mother to let me go to the concert. The first tool I'll try is flattery. If that doesn't work I'll use bribery, such as doing errands, clearing the dishes, washing the dishes, walking the dog, taking out the trash, mowing the lawn. If that doesn't work I'll threaten her with getting poor grades, dressing sloppily and not doing my homework, etc.

SITUATIONS:

1. Two sisters are having a disagreement in a motel on a freezing winter's night, and the heat does not seem to be working.

2. A father and son are having a confrontation about something the son has done of which the father disapproved. They are in car that ran out of gas on a cold, winter night.

3. Two boys are having a disagreement in a rustic cabin. Because of their argument, they have not even gotten a fire going yet, and it is snowing outside.

4. Two girls are having a disagreement about a boyfriend. They are sitting in a sauna.

5. A principal is having a conference in his office with a student who has broken a school rule. The school is not air conditioned, and it is 102 degrees outside.

6. A mother and daughter are having a disagreement about a boy the daughter is dating. They are standing on a sidewalk waiting for a bus, and it is over one hundred degrees out.

7. Two friends are having an argument about the stereo one lent to the other that got broke. They are watching a football game outdoors, and it is 17 degrees out.

8. A police officer has arrested a suspect who claims innocence. They are at police headquarters. Due to a power outage, there is no air conditioning and it is 105 degrees out.

9. A couple is disagreeing on whether they should be dating other people. They are at work in a meat locker where the temperature is kept at 28 degrees.

COACHING TIP: Did the students answer all off the Seven Ws? Do they know what the Seven Ws questions are? Were the students believable in the execution of the exercise? Did each student create the atmosphere of "hot" or "cold"? What could they have done to be more specific?

LESSON SIXTEEN

The Magnificent Seven Part III

Putting It Together

or

The Six Ws Plus the Seventh W: What do I have to do to get what I want?

OBJECTIVE: To think logically in breaking down a scene by answering the questions of the Seven Ws, creating moment-to-moment reality and dealing with the elements of conflict in an improvisational situation involving pain.

ACTIVITY: Two students engage in an improvisation. Select the two students and have them agree on the Seven Ws and who is to play which role. For each given situation, the improvisation is between an employer and an employee candidate. One student should select a specific condition that will emanate or reflect the condition of pain.

1. What is this scene about? A person interviewing for a summer job.

2. Who am I? A high school student.

3. Where am I? In a manager's office.

4. What am I doing? Sitting in a chair trying to look comfortable and confident.

5. What do I want? A summer job.

6. Why do I want it? To earn cash in order to buy a car next summer.

7. What do I have to do to obtain it? My action/task is to <u>persuade</u> the employer I can do the job. My tools are with <u>confidence, enthusiasm,</u> and <u>determination.</u>

SITUATIONS:

You are:

1. . . . interviewing for a pizza delivery job with a manager who has a toothache.

2. . . . interviewing for a drug store assistant job with an owner who has a thorbbing headache.

3. . . . interviewing for a clerk's position at a legal office with an attorney who has an itchy skin condition.

4. . . . interviewing at a fast food restaurant with a manager who has a bad back that makes shifting positions painful.

5. . . . interviewing at a Seven Eleven store with a manager who has a severe earache.

6. . . . nursing a painful broken shoulder while interviewing for a newspaper delivery job.

7. . . . interviewing for a job as telephone solicitor but you have a severe sore throat.

8. . . . interviewing for a job at an electronics store and the manager has a painful sprained ankle.

9. . . . interviewing for a job in a computer store and you have a severe stiff neck.

10. . . . interviewing for a job in a supermarket but you have something in your eye.

11. . . . interviewing for a job as a camp counselor to younger children but you are covered with hives from an allergic reaction to a beesting you got yesterday.

12. . . . interviewing for a job mowing lawns at an apartment complex but you are in pain and wearing a neck brace because you were in a car accident yesterday.

13. . . . interviewing for a job in a restaurant and the manager has severe hip pains.

14. . . . interviewing for a job as a warehouse clerk and you have a severe pain in your right wrist.

15. . . . interviewing for a job in an ice cream parlor and you have a severe upper back problem.

16. . . . interviewing for a job as a lifeguard and your left eye is painful and swollen and almost closed.

17. . . . interviewing for a job as an usher at a movie theatre and you are on crutches and in pain.

18. . . . interviewing for a job as an attendant at an amusement park and your left arm is in pain and in a cast.

19. . . . interviewing for a job in a bank and your fingers are in pain and swollen.

20. . . . interviewing for a job in a book store and you are in pain from a leg injury.

COACHING TIPS: Did the student use the Seven Ws? Was the pain realistic? Was the pain specific? Ask the class what they thought of the improvisation and if it was clear to them. Ask them if any of the Seven Ws were missing. Then give your own critique. Make sure the students address you and not the students doing the improvisation. Was the scene believable?

MONOLOGUES, SPEECHES
AND POETRY

LESSON SEVENTEEN

The First Eight Monologues

OBJECTIVE: To speak clearly and believably while understanding both the material and the reason for speaking.

ACTIVITY: Have the students select and memorize one or more of the following monologues to present to the class. Each student should answer the following questions concerning the material they have chosen:

1. Who am I? (Age, family background, etc.)

2. Where am I? (On stage? At the dinner table? In your room? Writing in your diary?)

3. Who am I speaking to? (Yourself? Your diary? Your parent? Your teacher? Your friend?)

4. What do I want? (To gain absolution? To get sympathy? To relate a funny tale? To be loved?)

5. What do I have to do to get it? (To plead for understanding? To be hurt or angry? To show you have been dealt an injustice?)

ALONE

Sometimes I feel so alone. Like there is no one who understands what I'm going through. I feel different, unimportant. I wish I knew someone else just like me. My parents tell me it's good not to be like everyone else. But I just want someone, anyone to understand.

PEACH WALLS

In my room, when I was growing up, all I remember was the way it was - peach walls, closet, desk, nightstand and two beds. I would always be in trouble for something; I can't even remember what some of the reasons were. After each incident I would always hear a long lecture from my parents. They would send me to my room and say to me, "Now, I want you to think about what you have done and how you feel about it." Well, I never would think. I would just sit and look at the peach walls and brown desk and white table. I would look and look until I could look no more. Then my parents would come and they would ask me for my answer and I could not tell them anything because all I could remember were the peach walls, the peach walls, the peach walls.

MY FIRST DANCE

I went to my first dance with the hope of dancing every dance with this special girl that I liked. I didn't know if she liked me. For that matter, I didn't really know if she knew I existed. Anyway, I thought she was pretty and I wanted her to dance only with me. Everyone from school was at the dance. The first dance began and I started looking for her. She was at the punch bowl. I walked over to the table. It was hard to look at her but I did and she smiled. She actually looked at me and smiled. I knew I had it made. I poured myself some punch, killing a little time so I could muster up enough nerve to ask her to dance with me. I thought, what if she didn't want to dance with me? Maybe she was just being polite when she smiled? Maybe she smiled at everyone? If she didn't dance with me, everyone would actually see her turn me down. What would I do then? I turned to look at her to see if she was still smiling. She wasn't there. She was already on the dance floor dancing with some other guy. I decided to go to her when the music stopped but my feet were like cement. I just couldn't get enough nerve to go to her and ask her for a dance. So I just stood there while other boys danced with her. I got jealous. Finally, I knew I just had to do it. I made up my mind to go to her, no matter what happened. Walking across the floor seemed to take forever. It was like going to China through peanut butter. As I took each heavy step across the floor I felt like the entire world was watching me. I was so nervous that I was shaking like I had some kind of strange affliction. I finally arrived. I could hardly speak. I asked her. She said yes. It was the best experience in my entire life. That was a long time ago and I don't dance with her anymore. She moved away. I think of her though. Mostly when I go to a dance. I'm not as shy as I was. But I don't think I've been so afraid in my life as I was the night of my first dance.

THE DAY I HAD TO GIVE UP MY DOG

When I was about seven, I wanted a dog. So my parents got me a tiny, three-week-old collie. She was one of the cutest pups I had ever seen and I loved her the minute I saw her. But we found out later that there was one thing wrong with her. She had a passion for chasing things. This passion grew, and her favorite things to chase were cars. We lived very close to a highway at the time, and she had many close calls. We were soon forced to tie her to a tree to prevent her from being killed. She was unhappy. I decided it would be best if I found somebody else to take care of her. But who? I placed ad after ad in the paper, but there was no response. One morning, my mom woke me up and told me a man was here to give my puppy a new home. I dressed as quickly as I could and ran out into the front yard. The man was lifting my dog into his truck. As my dad thanked the man, I hugged my dog goodbye. The man got into his truck and drove off. That Saturday morning, around 10:00 A.M., was the last time I ever saw my puppy dog. I never even knew the man's name.

MY BEST FRIEND

We did so many things together. Once I slept over at her house and we watched the movie "Grease." The next day we went to the record store and bought the "Grease" soundtrack. We played it all day, and we even wrote dialogue for in between songs. We would always fight over who would be Sandy. Another thing we would do was write letters to her parents saying if they let me sleep over we would be very good. We always played tricks on her older sister, like telling her bad news that wasn't true and making fun of her. We also made a clubhouse and had our own club. We made up rules and everything. Then one day I got some bad news. I was moving. I wouldn't be living next door to my best friend anymore. Now I would be living far away. But I thought at least I'll go to the same school. But I soon regretted that. At school there was a new girl who happened to have moved into my old house. My best friend and the new girl got to be best friends. They were always together. At school I would talk to them but they would ignore me. I finally realized that I had lost my best friend. Now and then, whenever I hear a song from the soundtrack of "Grease," I think about her. But not for very long. I have new friends now.

I HAD LONG HAIR ONCE

I had long hair once. Mom made me cut it off. I had long hair once. Long and flowing all the way down my back. Blonde rivers flowing, blowing in the wind. Can you see it? No, Mom made me cut it off. The rivers stopped flowing and blowing in the wind. Now I have just a pool. No streams, no rivers, no waves down my back. Just a little ripple reaching and stopping at my neck. I had long hair once but Mom made me cut it off.

MY FIRST ICE CREAM CONE

I remember when I was little, maybe two or three years old, I wanted an ice cream cone, my very first one. My mom said, "You'll drip it all over your new white dress." I said I wouldn't. I said I would be very, very careful. Well, what mom can refuse a little kid some ice cream? Especially her very first ice cream cone. Soon I had my very first ice cream cone in my little hands. Chocolate. As I put it in my little mouth it was smooth and creamy. It was the best thing I had every tasted! How could anything be so good, I asked myself. We finally arrived where we were going. I don't remember where. I was too busy with my chocolate ice cream cone. Suddenly, I was getting out of the car, still loving my ice cream, when all of a sudden the whole wonderful scoop fell down the front of my dress. "Oh, no!" I said to myself. Not only had I lost the delicious chocolate ice cream, but I had ruined my new white dress. I looked up at my mom, and I knew she would be upset. But she just smiled. What can I say? Mothers know best.

I LOVE

I love gumdrops and roses and chocolate chip cookies. Soft cuddly blankets and my cat named Snookies. I love rainbows, balloons and all living things. I love the Christmas spirit and the joy that it brings. I love the world we live in for its beautiful sight. I love the life I have and try to live it right.

COACHING TIPS: Did each student break down their monologue and answer the five Monologue Ws? Was the delivery sincere? Did each student create the illusion it was happening for the first time?

LESSON EIGHTEEN

The Last Seven Monologues

OBJECTIVE: To speak clearly and believably while understanding both the material and the reason for speaking.

ACTIVITY: Have the students select and memorize one or more of the following monologues to present to the class.

THE ESCALATOR

I can't remember how old I was, perhaps about ten years old. My mom, my brother, a friend and I went to the mall to get me some new shoes. Afterwards, I insisted on wearing my new red Keds. As we were going down the escalator my friend whispered something in my ear. Suddenly I looked down and saw that my shoe was caught in the crack of the escalator. I quietly informed my mother. My mother started screaming, "Somebody help, my baby's foot is caught in the escalator!" I was so embarrassed that my cheeks were the color of my new red Keds. My brother started crying because he was scared that it was going to tear my legs to shreds. When my mother stopped screaming, it seemed like everybody froze. Everyone just looked at my mother. Then someone from the crowd ran and pushed the emergency stop button. The escalator finally stopped. They carried me down like I was an invalid. I was so embarrassed. When we had taken my shredded shoe off, all my toes had big blisters on them. I soon recovered. What did I learn? I learned never to ride an escalator wearing new red Keds! Boy, what a trip!

A SECRET

My locker is across the hall, opposite from his. He isn't very tall. He's a go-getter. Not someone who waits. He doesn't expect everything on a plate. I know he likes me as a friend. But is that all? Is that the end? I smile and I flirt and he treats me like dirt. When I'm not there, does he care? What shall I do? What do I tell him? How will he know? I'm so confused. Any more of this pressure and I'll be depressed. This is a secret. I must never tell. If this gets out, if anyone finds out, I'm finished, I'm through. Oh God, I wish I knew what to do!

THE SOLUTION

Have you ever had a problem you just can't solve? Have you ever had a goal you just can't meet? Have you ever wished you couldn't feel defeat? If you ever have, just take a deep breath and try again!

CHEERLEADING

It was four o'clock in the afternoon. I was very nervous. It was my first time trying out for cheerleading. As I was standing at the door waiting for the judge to call my number, I was shaking. My hands were trembling, and I was very tense. I kept saying to myself "Don't be nervous, don't be nervous, don't be nervous." And then it happened. The judge called my number. I was so scared. I did my chant and my cheers and then sat down and waited for the other people in my group to do theirs. As I was sitting I knew I had done very badly. After everyone had gone we all went out into the hall and waited for the judges to come out and tell us who made it. Ten minutes passed but they had not decided. Finally, they came out and put the numbers on a piece of poster board. I looked frantically for my number. But my number was not there. My number was nowhere to be found on the poster. I waited to see if there had been a mistake but the numbers never changed. I felt awful! I wanted to burst into tears, but I kept them inside. That week, every time someone mentioned cheerleading, I wanted to yell at them. I just couldn't concentrate on my school work all week. That was a terrible, horrible week. . . the week I didn't make the cheerleading squad. Oh, well, there's always next time.

MY SISTER AND I

My sister and I always fight, but not as much as we used to. We fight about who should feed the pets or who has to unload the dishwasher. We even fight about what radio station we should listen to in the car. Sometimes, when we are fighting, my mother will come and fight with us. My sister will be going to college soon. She will be far away. No more fighting over the dishes, radio stations or pets. I'll miss her.

MY WORST DAY

This has been the worst day of my life. I mean really bad! First of all, my alarm didn't go off on time this morning. I overslept by half an hour. I didn't have enough time to get ready for school 'cause my mom had to leave for work. When I got to school my friends were mad at me 'cause I was in a bad mood. When I went to my history class, we got a major test back. I had studied and I really thought I did a good job but, oh no, I failed it and my teacher said he was gonna send me a warning slip. The worst of it, when I finally got home, my mom and I got in a really big fight, but I forgot what it was all about. Now as I'm about to fall asleep I can only pray that tomorrow will be another day. A better day.

GOING OUT ON A LIMB

I'll never forget the first time I was attracted to a girl. There was a new girl in the neighborhood. She lived in the big two-story house on the corner of the block where I lived. She was a blonde with blue eyes. Someone told me she had her own room. She didn't have to share her room because she didn't have any brothers or sisters. In the afternoon she would sit out on her porch—usually on the porch step—and her mother would sit in a rocker. She would do her homework while her mother would read some kind of paper or magazine. My two friends and I played in the tree across the street from where she lived. I wondered what would happen if I just went up to her and said hello and told her who I was and where I lived. I was so afraid that she would walk into the house. I was so afraid that my friends would see me turned away. I was so afraid of being rejected and being hurt. I don't know why I wanted to meet her. I only knew I had to meet her and talk with her. We would play Tarzan and swing on the limbs and make wise-cracks, kidding around so she could hear us. I knew she could hear us because I would see her smile sometimes. She had to be the prettiest girl I had ever seen. I wanted her to look at me in the worst way. So one day I announced that I would jump from limb to limb without using my hands. I had tried it alone one day and wanted to surprise my friends and the girl. I jumped to the first limb and then the second. I was pretty high in the tree. I looked out of the corner of my eye and saw that the pretty blue-eyed blonde was watching me for the first time. I decided to leap to the next limb, but then the bark came off where I placed my foot and down I went to the ground. My wrist was caught behind my back and I fell on it. I started to cry and the girl leaped up and ran across the street to where I had fallen. She asked if I was all right. I tried to stop crying but I couldn't. I looked at her and just shook my head. She touched my wrist. I continued to cry as I looked at her. She was the most beautiful girl I had ever seen. She said that her mother was getting help. Later, I was taken to the hospital, and they put a cast on the wrist. I had broken it. I never went back to the tree or bothered to show off again for the girl. I was too embarrassed. She moved away. Not too long after, our family moved into the big house where she lived. I had my own room. I often wondered if it was her room. I wondered if she was as nice as she was pretty. I often wonder what would have happened if I just simply walked up to her and introduced myself.

COACHING TIPS: Did each student break down their monologues and answer the five Monologue Ws? Was the delivery sincere? Did each student create the illusion it was happening for the first time?

LESSON NINETEEN

Bow Wow - A Tribute To A Dog

An Impassioned Speech

OBJECTIVE: To apply the Seven Ws in the delivery of a speech.

ACTIVITY: Students should choose one of the following given circumstances and incorporate the following Seven Ws:

> What is the scene about?
>
> Who am I?
>
> Where am I?
>
> What am I doing?
>
> What do I want?
>
> Why do I want it?
>
> What do I have to do to get it?

1. You are a lawyer trying to win a case for the plaintiff at a trial involving a dog.

2. You are awarding a medal to a dog at a school assembly for a heroic act that involved a fellow student.

3. You are at a national speech contest and there is a college scholarship for the winner.

4. You are giving the speech to a judge and jury who are thinking about putting the dog to sleep because he attacked someone. You know the dog is good.

Tribute To A Dog

In this world of ours, a man's own brother may turn against him and become his enemy. His son or daughter, whom he has reared with loving care, may prove ungrateful. Those who are nearest and dearest to us, those whom we trust with our happiness and our good name, may become traitors to their faith. The money that a man has, he may lose. It flies away from him, perhaps when he needs it most. A man's reputation may be sacrificed in a moment of ill-considered action. The people who are prone to fall on their knees to do us honor when success is with us may be the ones to cast the first stones of malice when failure settles its cloud upon our heads. The one absolutely unselfish friend that man can have in this selfish world, the one which never deserts him, the one which never proves ungrateful or treacherous, is his dog. A man's dog stands by him in prosperity and in poverty, in health and in sickness. He will sleep on the cold ground, where the wintry winds blow and the snow drives fiercely, if only he may be near his master's side. He will kiss the hand that has no food to offer; he will lick the wounds and sores that come from encounters with the roughness of the world. He guards the sleep of his pauper master as if he were a prince. When all other friends desert, he remains. When riches take wing, and reputation falls to pieces, he is as constant in his love as the sun in its journey through the heavens.

If fortune drives the master forth, an outcast in the world, friendless and homeless, the faithful dog asks no higher privilege than that of accompanying him, to guard him against danger, to fight against his enemies. And when the last scene of all comes, and death takes his master in its embrace and his body is laid away in the cold ground, no matter if all other friends pursue their way, there by the grave side will the noble dog be found, watchful, faithful and true even in death.

COACHING TIPS: Did the student answer all the Seven Ws? Was the student believable? Have the student describe the dog. If he cannot, have the student describe a dog he knows or make up a description of a dog to base the story upon.

LESSON TWENTY

How Now Brown Cow?

Poetry

OBJECTIVE: To appreciate and understand the various forms of great poetry and to develop skills as an oral reader.

ACTIVITY: The student should read the following excerpt and poem aloud in front of the class.

THE BELLS

by Edgar Alan Poe

Hear the sledges with the bells,

Silver bells!

What a world of merriment their melody foretells!

How they tinkle, tinkle, tinkle,

In the icy air of night!

While the stars, that over sprinkle

All the heavens, seem to twinkle

With a crystalline delight;

Keeping time, time, time,

In a sort of Runic rhyme,

To the tintinnabulation that so musically wells

From the bells, bells, bells,

Bells, bells, bells -

From the jingling and the tinkling of the bells.

II

Hear the mellow wedding bells,

Golden bells!

What a world of happiness their harmony foretells!

Through the balmy air of night

How they ring out their delight!

From the molten-golden notes,

And all in tune,

What a liquid ditty floats

To the turtle-dove that listens, while she gloats

On the moon!
Oh, from out the sounding cells,
What a gush of euphony voluminously wells!
How it swells!
How it dwells
On the future! How it tells
Of the rapture that impels
To the swinging and the ringing
Of the bells, bells, bells,
Of the bells, bells, bells, bells,
Bells, bells, bells-
To the rhyming and the chiming of the bells!

CASEY AT THE BAT

by Ernest Lawrence Thayer

The outlook wasn't brilliant for the Mudville nine that day;
The score stood four to two, with but one inning left to play.
So, when Cooney died at second, and Burrow did the same,
A pallor wreathed the features of the patrons of the game.

A straggling few got up to go in deep despair. The rest
Clung to the hope which springs eternal within the human breast;
They thought, "If only Casey could get a whack at that -
We'd put up even money now, with Casey at the bat."

But Flynn preceded Casey, as did also Jimmy Blake,
And the former was a lulu, and the latter was a fake,
So upon that stricken multitude a deathlike silence sat,
For there seemed but little chance of Casey's getting to the bat.

But Flynn let drive a single, to the wonderment of all,
And Blake, the much despised, tore the cover off the ball;
And when the dust had lifted, and they saw what had occurred,
There was Jimmy safe at second and Flynn a-hugging third.
Then from five thousand throats and more there rose a lusty yell;
It rumbled in the mountain tops, it rattled in the dell;
It struck upon the hillside and recoiled on the flat;
For Casey, mighty Casey, was advancing to the bat.

There was ease in Casey's manner as he stepped into his place;
There was pride in Casey's bearing and a smile on Casey's face.
And when, responding to the cheers, he lightly doffed his hat,
No stranger in the crowd could doubt 'twas Casey at the bat.

Ten thousand eyes were on him as he rubbed his hands with dirt;
Five thousand tongues applauded when he wiped them on his shirt.
Then while the writhing pitcher ground the ball into his hip,
Defiance gleamed in Casey's eye, a sneer curled Casey's lip.

And now the leather-covered sphere came hurling through the air,
And Casey stood a-watching it in haughty grandeur there.
Close by the sturdy batsman the ball unheeded sped-
"That ain't my style," said Casey - "Strike one," the Umpire said.
From the benches, black with people, there went up a muffled roar,
Like the beating of storm-waves on a stern and distant shore.
"Kill him! Kill the umpire!" shouted someone on the stand;
And it's likely they'd have killed him had not Casey raised a hand.
With a smile of Christian charity great Casey's visage shone;
He stilled the rising tumult; he bade the game go on;
He signaled to the pitcher, once more the spheroid flew;
But Casey still ignored it, and the Umpire said, "Strike two."

"Fraud!" cried the maddened thousands, and echo answered,
"Fraud!"
But one scornful look from Casey and the multitude was awed.
They saw his face grow stern and cold, they saw his muscles strain,
And they knew that Casey wouldn't let that ball go by again.

The sneer is gone from Casey's lip, his teeth are clenched in hate;
He pounds with cruel violence his bat upon the plate.
And now the pitcher holds the ball, and now he lets it go,
And now the air is shattered by the force of Casey's blow.

Oh, somewhere in this favored land the sun is shining bright;
The band is playing somewhere, and somewhere hearts are light,
And somewhere men are laughing, and somewhere children shout;
But there is no joy in Mudville - mighty Casey has struck out.

COACHING TIPS: What is the author's intent? How does he accomplish it? What makes the poem unique? Did the student create the appropriate mood for the content? Was the student's diction clear?

LESSON TWENTY-ONE

Now Hear This!

Solo Impromptu Speech

OBJECTIVE: To speak clearly and forcefully by organizing thoughts while thinking on your feet, remembering to concentrate on ideas as they are put into words.

ACTIVITY: Each student must act as an expert on a subject and do an impromptu speech based on one of the five following subjects. Absolutely no preparation time. After the student chooses his subject he then chooses his audience from the ten groups listed below.

SUBJECTS:

1. The legalization of drugs

2. The right of every student to attend the school of his/her choice

3. The need for socialized medicine

4. The need to ban smoking

5. The need for the death penalty

AUDIENCE:

1. Hearing Impaired class

2. Kindergarten class

3. Group of teachers

4. Juvenile delinquents

5. Retired citizens

6. Clergymen

7. Visiting firemen from Japan

8. Cowboys from Texas

9. Drug addicts

10. Convicted killers

COACHING TIPS: Each actor must believe his speech and must take it seriously. Let the rest of the class prepare questions for the speaker to answer.

LESSON TWENTY-TWO

More Best-Selling Authors

Solo Impromptu Speech with Group Participation

OBJECTIVE: To use the imagination to create a believable monologue, remembering to speak clearly and forcefully by organizing thoughts and to concentrate on ideas as they are put into words.

ACTIVITY: Each student must act as an expert on a subject and do an impromptu address based on a recent best-seller she has authored. There shoulb be absolutely no preparation time. Students have written such great books as:

1. The Joy of Being Twelve Feet Tall: A Pill That Works

2. Changing Life Styles: A Credit Card for All Ages with No Cash Limit

3. Alternative Transportation: Roller Blades

4. Incognito: My Life As A Dog

5. Alternative Housing: Living on a House Boat

6. Exotic Mode of Transportation: By Rocket Pack

7. Past Lives:

        A. I Was Once a Soldier in the Civil War

        B. I Was Once a Pirate

        C. I Was Once a Gladiator

        D. I Was Once a Princess

8. Kidnapped by Aliens: I Was Kidnapped and Interrogated for Two Hours in a Space Ship

9. The Summer I Spent in a Tree House with a Family of Chimpanzees

10. Alternative Transportation: Giant Turtles

COACHING TIPS: Each student should speak for three or more minutes. Afterwards, open the discussion to get the students to make positive comments or suggestions to improve individual speakers. Was the speaker convincing? Did the speaker concentrate as she spoke? Have the students interview the author after each speech.

LESSON TWENTY-THREE

More Memory Lane

Solo Impromptu Speech

OBJECTIVE: To imagine and create a vivid scene that happened in the past with the emphasis on believability.

ACTIVITY: Describe the time...

1. ...you took a trail ride with a group of cowboys.

2 ...you joined a group of anti-war marchers.

3. ...you were captured and examined in a spaceship by aliens.

4. ...you were kidnapped by a band of pirates.

5. ...you were on a plane that ran out of fuel.

6. ...you won an apple pie eating contest.

7. ...you were in trouble and were saved by a troop of Girl Scouts.

8. ...you participated in the Olympic Games on the moon.

9. ...you met a rock star.

10. ...you lived with a tribe of Indians.

11. ...you drove a car for the first time.

12. ...your dog first talked to you.

13. ...you jumped out of a plane with an umbrella.

14. ...you got lost in the desert.

15. ...the police arrested you for something you did not do. A case of mistaken identity.

16. ...you worked at Disneyland one summer.

17. ...you fell overboard from a boat.

18. ...you received a personal telephone call from an astronaut on the space shuttle.

19. ...you met the President of the United States.

20. ...you were on a sinking ship.

COACHING TIPS: Was the scene real? Did the student rely on words alone? Was the presentation smooth? Talk about storytelling techniques such as having a beginning, a middle and an end, setting the scene, using creative, vivid words and creating suspense.

PANTOMIME

LESSON TWENTY-FOUR

What Does It All Mean?

Justifying Physical Activities

OBJECTIVE: To be able to justify specific physical activities as an introduction to pantomime.

ACTIVITY: Three actors join in executing the set of physical activities in the order listed. Improvisational dialogue may be used.

1. Turning on the television
    Eating
    Drinking
    Jumping up and down

2. Slapping someone on the face
    Crying
    Laughing
    Falling on your knees

3. Fainting on the floor
    Kissing someone's hand
    Getting dizzy
    Fainting on the floor again

4. Playing
    Crying
    Limping
    Sipping a drink

5. Running in circles
    Smoking
    Laughing
    Sleeping

COACHING TIPS: Did the students make believable transitions into each physical activity? Did the students do each physical activity believably?

LESSON TWENTY-FIVE

Howdy, Partner!

Partner Pantomimes

OBJECTIVE: To be specific with a chosen physical activity.

ACTIVITY: Both students use a sequence of physical activities to depict the activity they are performing. The class can guess the activity as the students simultaneously perform the physical activity.

1. a. Walk fast (in place)
    b. Walk slow (in place)

2. a. Write with a pen
    b. Write with a pencil

3. a. Wash your face
    b. Dry your face

4. a. Enter a room
    b. Exit a room

5. a. Chop wood
    b. Play baseball

6. a. Impersonate a king
    b. Impersonate a queen

7. a. Eat lunch
    b. Drink a beverage

8. a. Mow the lawn
    b. Cut the hedges

9. a. Brush your teeth
    b. Comb your hair

10. a. Decorate a cake
    b. Make a salad

COACHING TIPS: Did the students use separate and distinct physical activities? For instance, the student writing with the pen might have picked up the pen and taken the cover off (or used her thumb to push the top of the pen down so the point was ready for use if it was a ball point pen). Did the student writing with a pencil check the point and sharpen the pencil first? The critical element is that the student must make it clear as to what she is doing.

LESSON TWENTY-SIX

Tell It Like It Is!

Justification Pantomimes

OBJECTIVE: To justify movement and to stimulate the imagination by executing specific gestures and movements.

ACTIVITY: Each student is assigned one of the following physical activities to do in pantomime.

EXAMPLE: Putting your hands to your head: As if you were saying "Turn off the siren, I can't stand it any more!" Kneeling: You are playing football or being knighted. You also can be kneeling in a Catholic Church, or helping a wounded animal, or petting a cat.

1. Enter stage right, cross to the center stage and kneel.

2. Enter stage right, cross to center stage and raise both hands.

3. Enter stage right, cross to center stage and scratch your head.

4. Enter stage right, cross to center stage, kneel; then get up and raise your hand.

5. Enter stage right, cross to center stage and sit; then roll over.

6. Enter stage right, cross to center, put your hands on your hips, scratch your head, then raise both arms over your head.

7. Enter stage right, cross to center stage, pat your tummy, wipe your mouth, then lay down.

8. Enter stage right and cross to center stage, put both hands on your hips and shake your head.

9. Enter stage right and cross to center stage, put both hands on hips and shake your head.

10. Enter stage right and cross to center stage, raise one arm over your head then lower it, and then raise the other arm over your head and then lower it, then raise and extend both arms to your sides.

COACHING TIPS: Have the class guess what the actor's gestures indicate. If the gestures that were executed by the students were not as clear as the student would have liked them to be, ask the class what could be done to have made them clearer and more specific. Always compliment and encourage the student who is performing. You don't want the student to feel incompetent or untalented and therefore become an unwilling participant.

LESSON TWENTY-SEVEN
So You're An Actor
Body Language

OBJECTIVE: To incorporate movement with body control to convey meaning while creating a specific character and performing a single pantomime.

ACTIVITY: Each student will select a role from the list below and, by simply walking across the room, suggest the type of character she has chosen. Each student should be able to explain what physical characteristics distinguish each.

EXAMPLE: A custodian: A person who works as a custodian may be pushing a utility cart, stopping to empty wastebaskets, dust or sweep the floor. She may also carry tools to make small repairs, such as on a light fixture or door.

Roles:

1. A girl with her first high heels

2. A panhandler

3. President of the United States

4. A person with motion sickness on a boat

5. A prize-fighter

6. A blind person

7. A waiter/waitress

8. A snob

9. An invalid

10. A drunk

11. A bully

12. A meticulous person

13. A wrestler

14.   A model

15. A deer hunter

16. An athlete

17.   A cheerleader

18.   A teacher

19.   A lion tamer

20.   A police officer

COACHING TIPS: Did each student convey a meaning while creating a simple character? Was each student specific? Ask the student what physical characteristics distinguished his character. Ask the students who were watching what they thought of the choices and the results of the excercise. Have the students direct the questions to you, the teacher, and not to the student performing.

LESSON TWENTY-EIGHT

What State Is This?

Solo Pantomime Game

OBJECTIVE: To strengthen the imagination and the sense of communication through pantomime.

ACTIVITY: Each student is given a name of a state in the United States and acts out a physical activity to give a clue to the name of the state. For instance, to act out Connecticut, a student could connect a series of pipes and then pantomime cutting with scissors. As the coach, ask the students what the actor is doing. Stop the actor if necessary and privately tell him how to be more specific with his pantomime gestures.

1. Texas (cowboys or longhorns)

2. Mississippi (baseball player at bat swinging and missing the ball or someone sipping a soda)

3. Arkansas (Noah and his ark or sawing wood)

4. Hawaii (Hula dancers; climbing up a coconut tree and breaking a coconut after coming down the tree; drinking the juice and eating the coconut fruit)

5. Oregon (man in a boat with oars)

6. Alaska (man and his dog sled or being very, very cold)

7. Indiana (an Indian performing a rain dance or shooting with a bow and arrow)

8. Washington (washing clothes or washing your face or your car)

9. Massachusetts (going to Mass at a Catholic church; kneeling and taking holy water and blessing oneself)

10. Kentucky (tuck in your shirt)

By the end of session working with the ten states listed above, the student should be able to come up with his own.

COACHING TIPS: Guide the class by asking what the performer is trying to communicate. If he is tucking in his shirt to elicit the response of Kentucky, ask the class, "What is he doing?" or "What is he doing with his shirt?" If they say "Putting on his shirt!", you say, "What is another way of saying that?" Keep going until they say "tucking," then ask for the state's name! Remind the students that there are two ways to give a clue about a state -- they can either act out a characteristic for a state (such as a hula dance for Hawaii) or they can break down the name of the state and try to act out a certain part or word within the name (as in "tuck" for Kentucky).

BLOCKING

LESSON TWENTY-NINE

I Want To Be Moved!

Solo Blocking: One Move

OBJECTIVE: To motivate a blocking direction, justify a physical activity and understand the use of an action/task and of tools, demonstrating an awareness that there must be a reason for all movement on stage.

ACTIVITY: Each student will cross from Stage Right to Center Stage. When you have the first studend cross ask, "Why did you just do that?" The answer from the student should be, "Because you told me to!" Congratulate the student for taking direction and justifying it. Each student should now be invited to justify his movement to Center Stage. The teacher should tell the student the situation, action/task and possible tools to use from the list below.

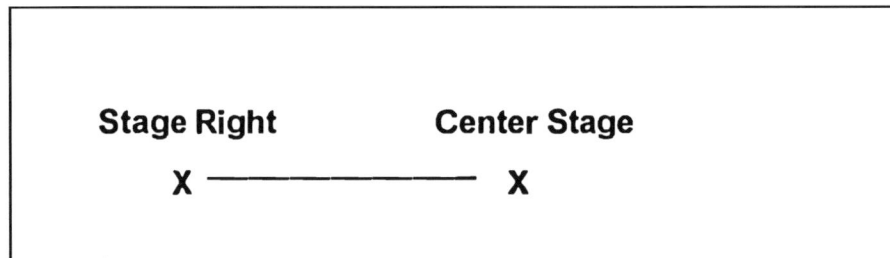

```
┌─────────────────────────────────────────────────┐
│                                                 │
│    Stage Right         Center Stage             │
│       X ───────────────── X                     │
│                                                 │
└─────────────────────────────────────────────────┘
```

Ask each student to cross from Stage Right to Center Stage using one of the following justifications:

1. You go to Center Stage to wait for a bus. (Where are you going? Why are you going?)

Action/Task: You are late for class and you want to get on the bus because your class is going on a field trip today. You may be the student left behind and you will have to go to study hall all day.

Possible Tools: With anxiety, arrogance, anger

2. You go to Center Stage to cross the street but there is a red light and you must wait. (Where are you going? Why are you going?)

Action/Task: You want to cross the street because you want to talk with an old friend you haven't seen for a long time who is anxiously waving at you from across the street.

Possible tools: With enthusiasm, excitement, anxiety, joy.

3. You go to Center Stage to the river bank. (Why are you going there?)

Action/Task: You are at the river to have a picnic and swimming party with your friends.

Possible Tools: With excitement, relief, enthusiasm, calmness, joy.

4. You go to Center Stage because you just made a hole in one on the golf course. (Who is with you?)

You are golfing with your boss for the first time, and he is standing Center Stage to congratulate you.

Possible tools: With excitement, happiness, joy, embarrassment.

5. You go to Center Stage because you have just discovered it is a great place to fish. (Why are you fishing?)

Action/Task: You need to get food because you are hungry and lost in the woods.

Possible tools: With intensity, excitement, anticipation, enthusiasm.

6. You go to Center Stage because that is the spot where you can see the parade. (Why are you there? What kind of a parade is it?)

Action/Task: You want to get a glimpse of a rock star or a movie star you admire.

Possible tools: With excitement, anticipation, joyful expectation, frustration.

7. You go to Center Stage because you just found your seat at the concert. (Why are you going? What kind of a concert is it? Who is playing?)

Action/Task: It is your first time at a symphony, and the concert is about to begin.

Possible tools: With excitement, anticipation, happiness, dread, boredom.

8. You go to Center Stage because you heard a voice cry from inside the well. (Why are you going?)

Action/Task: You want to find out where the voice is coming from and whose it is.

Possible Tools: With curiosity, anxiety, fear, concern.

COACHING TIPS: Did each student justify his movements from Stage Right to Center Stage? Did he understand his motivation? Did he use his tools? Was it believable?

HOMEWORK SUGGESTION: Have each student bring in a solo blocking (one move) with a defined situation, an action/task and possible tools to use.

LESSON THIRTY

Move Me Again and Again! Part I

Solo Blocking: Two Moves

OBJECTIVE: To justify a physical activity and to exercise the notion that there must be a reason for all movement on stage.

ACTIVITY: Each student crosses from Stage Right to Stage Left, turns and crosses to Center Stage and sits. As before, each student should have a clear motivation, action/task and tool in mind before beginning.

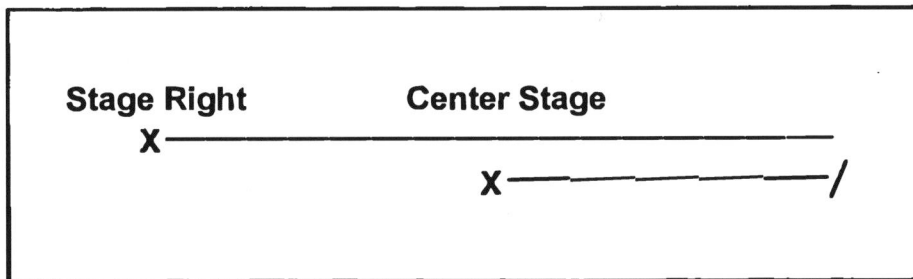

```
┌─────────────────────────────────────────────────┐
│                                                   │
│   Stage Right          Center Stage               │
│       X────────────────────────────────────       │
│                        X──────────────────/       │
│                                                   │
└─────────────────────────────────────────────────┘
```

EXAMPLE: You enter Stage Right and cross to Stage Left, pick up the T.V. changer, return to Center Stage, sit and begin to flip stations until you find the specific program you are looking for.

1. You go to get your homework and then return to your seat to study.

2. You go to select an audio cassette and then put it in a cassette player.

3. You go to prepare a snack and then proceed to sit down and eat it.

4. You're in a library. You select a book from the shelf and then return to your seat and read it.

5. You go to close the window because it is cold and then return to sit by the fire.

6. You go to get a file from a cabinet and then return to your desk to work on the material.

7. You go and pick up a musical instrument and then return to your seat and play it.

8. You take a picture in a frame off the wall, cross back with it to the chair where you will sit to change the picture in the frame.

9. You go and get some paper then sit down and put it into the computer printer or typewriter.

COACHING TIPS: Did each student justify her movements to Stage Right and Center Stage? Did she understand her motivation? Was it believable?

HOMEWORK SUGGESTION: Have each student bring in a solo blocking (two moves) with a defined situation, an action/task and possible tools to use.

LESSON THIRTY-ONE

Move Me Again and Again! Part II

Solo Blocking: Two Moves with Justification

OBJECTIVE: To justify a physical activity, exercising the notion that there must be a reason for all movement on stage, and demonstrating inner motivation or justification that will involve the actor emotionally.

ACTIVITY: Each student crosses from Stage Right to Stage Left, turns and crosses to Center Stage and sits. Remind the student to have a motivation, an action/task and a tool in mind before beginning.

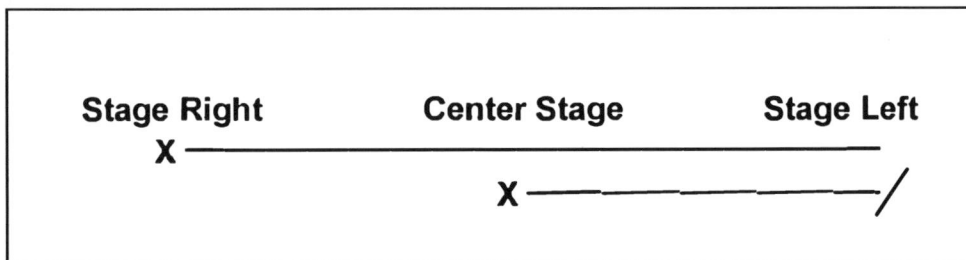

Stage Right	Center Stage	Stage Left
X ———————————————		
	X ——————————————/	

EXAMPLE: You enter Stage Right and cross to Stage Left, pick up the T.V. changer, return to Center Stage, sit and begin to flip stations until you find the specific program you are looking for.

1. You go and get silverware, then return to sit down and polish it.

JUSTIFICATION: You must do this chore before you are allowed to leave the house to participate in a social event that you are involved in and you are already late for the event.

2. You go and get some sewing material and garments, then return to your sofa, sit down and mend the garment.

JUSTIFICATION: You have a date with the best looking guy in school and you are fixing your special dress for the dance he has invited you to.

3. You go and get a pair of shoes, return to your seat and polish them.

JUSITFICATION: You are told to polish your gross looking shoes before wearing them to a wedding of an uncle whoyou do hardly know. You go and get some stationery, return to your desk and write a letter to someone special.

5. You go to the door and get a pizza that is delivered then bring it back to the table, sit down and eat.

JUSTIFICATION: You haven't had pizza for six months because you have been away in a small village in Alaska eating whale blubber and Eskimo pies.

6. You go to the refrigerator and pour a glass of milk then return to the table, sit down and continue eating your meal.

JUSTIFICATION: Your doctor has told you that you have a calcium deficiency and must drink several glasses of milk each day. You do not like milk.

7. You go to get a disk to bring back to your computer, put it in and bring up the program you are seeking.

JUSTIFICATION: The disk you are retrieving is a very special disk that has the answers to many problems you are dealing with. The disk is an object to covet.

8. You go and open the window to get some fresh air in the room and go back to continue your studying at the table.

JUSTIFICATION: You smell gas, look around to try and find out where the gas is coming from. Then you are forced to open the window.

9. You go to the pantry and get some dog snacks for your dog, bring them to the chair and call him in.

JUSTIFICATION: You are getting the snacks to reward your dog for his excellent response to your training session. He has just learned to sit, stay and come to you on command.

10. You go and make a peanut butter and jelly sandwich then return to your chair and eat it as you continue to watch T.V.

JUSTIFICATION: You are extremely hungry but are engrossed in an exciting action flick. You want the sandwich but don't want to miss any of the movie either.

COACHING TIPS: Did the students justify their movements to Stage Right and Center Stage? Did they understand their motivation? Was their justification believable? Was each student emotionally involved? Was it believable?

HOMEWORK SUGGESTION: Have each student bring in a solo blocking (two moves) with motivation and one physical action with justification.

LESSON THIRTY-TWO

Move The Two of Us!

Duet Blocking

OBJECTIVE: To justify specific blocking directions for two actors.

ACTIVITY: An improvisation for two students. Student B is discovered seated Center Stage. Student A enters Stage Right and goes to the right of student B. Student B rises and exits Stage Left. Student A sits in chair. They should use dialogue.

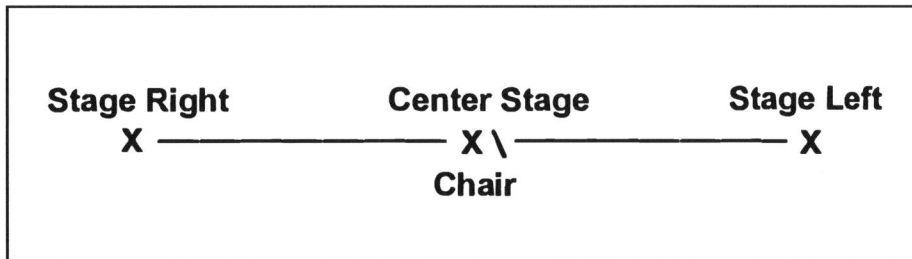

```
Stage Right          Center Stage          Stage Left
    X ————————————————— X \ ——————————————— X
                        Chair
```

Each pair of students should execute the above blocking in one of the following situations:

1. The friend that you are visiting has just received a phone call and has been instructed to inform you to go home immediately because a member of your family has just been injured.

2. Your mother asks you what you would like for dinner. You then get up and go out to the store for a missing ingredient.

3. Your father reminds you to take out the trash.

4. Your mother asks you to get off the phone because she needs to use it.

5. Your father reminds you to help your mother with the dishes.

6. Your mother asks you to bring in some firewood.

7. Your mother asks you to go up and clean your room.

8. You dad asks you to wash the car.

9. Your mom asks you to vacuum the rugs.

10. Your father asks you to help your brother paint the garage.

COACHING TIPS: Was enough dialogue used? Were the dialogue and blocking natural? Did each student justify his movements? Did he understand his motivation? Did he use his tools? Was it believable?

RELAXATION

LESSON THIRTY-THREE
Relax, Relax, Relax
Group Relaxation Exercise

OBJECTIVE: To totally relax the instrument (body) before beginning work.

ACTIVITY: Students sit in chairs, or, if possible, lie on the floor, as instructor guides them through the relaxation.

Suggestions for the instructor:

If you are not familiar with relaxation exercises, you may want to consult some psychology texts or exercise books before beginning. Have the students close their eyes and begin concentrating on their breathing. When you breathe properly, the abdomen and rib cage will expand as you inhale through your nose. On a exhalation, your diaphragm moves upward, compressing the lungs and pushing the air out. You may want to have the students breathe in, hold the breath, then exhale, repeating this several times. Follow this by guiding them through tensing and relaxing different muscles. Begin at either the feet or the head and work through the body. For example, start with the toes and have the students tense their toes, hold, then release. Then move up the legs, to the hips and abdomen, fingers, arms, chest and shoulders and finally the neck and head, tensing and relaxing each muscle group in turn. Make sure the process is slow and that the students are becoming more and more relaxed as they progress. Keep reminding them to breath gently and slowly. This exercise should take about fifteen minutes. When you are finished, allow the students to take their time "coming to." Say something like, "Remember this feeling of relaxation, all the tension gone from your body. When you feel ready, you can open your eyes."

COACHING TIPS: The instructor should move about the classroom and check each student, making sure they are relaxing and concentrating.

THE SENSES

LESSON THIRTY-FOUR

The Five Senses

Group and Solo Improvisations

OBJECTIVE: To sharpen the five senses and to strengthen concentration.

ACTIVITY: Emphasizing the five senses, a student should respond to the following situations and conditions:

1. TOUCH

   A. Pass a chunk of ice around the room

   B. Pass a hot skillet around the room

   C. Pass a fur coat around the room and feel the fur

2. HEARING

   A. Hear a police siren coming from a distance and arriving at your door

   B. Hear a mouse in the wall of a house

   C. Hear the sound of a dripping faucet

3. SIGHT

   A. See a tornado approaching you

   B. See a tractor trailer jack-knifing on the highway

   C. See a building collapse from an earthquake

4. TASTE

   A. Taste a spoonful of mustard

   B. Taste a spoonful of maple syrup

   C. Taste a bite out of a lemon

5. SMELL

   A. Smell leaves burning

   B. Smell an apple pie baking

C. Smell carnations, roses, violets

COACHING TIPS: Did the student use specific behavior to communicate to the audience what activity she was doing? Was she believable?

LESSON THIRTY-FIVE

The Egg and I

Solo Improvisation With All Five Senses

OBJECTIVE: To strengthen the five senses.

ACTIVITY: Each student assumes the role of a newly hatched chick entering the world for the first time.

Suggested Sequences:

1. Cracking the egg and entering the world

2. Adjusting the eyes to the light

3. Discovering and examining fingers, hands and arms

4. Discovering and examining toes, feet and legs

5. Discovering eye sockets, mouth cavity, nose and ear cavities

6. Discovering the hair on the head

7. Discovering how to stand, walk, hop, skip and jump, sit and crawl

COACHING TIPS: Guide the student through the various steps. Did the student create the illusion of the first time? Was he believable? Were the discoveries real and truthful?

THE MAGIC "IF"

LESSON THIRTY-SIX

Making It Real

The Magic "If"

OBJECTIVE: To create the proper mood in a scene by substituting a personal experience.

ACTIVITY: Each student should attempt to recreate the emotions associated with one of the following scenarios and then say the following line: My friend was in an accident. He died today. I will miss him.

What is it like dealing with the death of a loved one? The student may never have dealt with it before and therefore have no frame of reference. However, what is the emotion that goes along with the loss of a loved one? It is a <u>great</u> sense of loss. The loss of something of <u>great</u> value. Before entering the scene, tell the student to try and create the experience of a loss.

Such as the loss of...

1. ...an item of value you have lost.

2. ...a pet you loved who died or ran away.

3. ...a job you really liked and lost.

4. ...a position on a successful athletic team which you lost to someone else.

5. ...a friendship you cherished and valued.

6. ...a boyfriend or a girlfriend who meant a great deal to you.

IMPORTANT: Before performing, take a moment and silently try to experience the loss by imagining the feelings that accompany the given circumstances of the incident. Once you are feeling those emotions, then enter the scene and deliver the line.

COACHING TIPS: Was the emotion of loss clearly and specifically demonstrated? What kind of problems did each student encounter as she said her lines?

OBSERVATION

LESSON THIRTY-SEVEN

Try To Remember

Observation Skills

OBJECTIVE: To sharpen observation skills.

ACTIVITY: Students will be placed in situations that require them to observe and then report on their observations.

Situations:

1. Place two chairs facing one another. Have two students sit in the chairs and observe one another. Allow about two minutes.

   A. Turn the chairs back to back, and ask the same students to now sit in the chairs facing away from each other.

   B. Ask each student the following questions:

      1. Describe the color of the other student's eyes.
      2. Describe the color of the other student's hair.
      3. Describe how the other is dressed.
      4. Describe the jewelry each is wearing.

2. Bring in a tray of various items such as a wallet, a stapler, scotch tape, keys, glasses. Use about 10-12 items or as many as will fit on the tray. Have the class observe them for three minutes then place the tray out of sight. Have each student write the items down on a slip of paper and then read the results.

3. The instructor should stand behind the class and ask the class to describe what she or he is wearing.

4. The students should close their eyes and describe the room they are in. They should include the number of windows, number and color of chairs, etc.

COACHING TIPS: Did the students concentrate? Were they specific? Have the class describe what you are wearing several days in a row to encourage them to increase their power of observation.

IMPROVISATIONS AND
THEATRE GAMES

LESSON THIRTY-EIGHT

Get Thee To A Mall

Selecting Verbs For Action/Tasks

OBJECTIVE: To use active verbs for selected action/tasks.

ACTIVITY: Two students should perform a simple improvisation using active verbs from the list to achieve a given goal.

EXAMPLE: You want to go to the mall with a friend and your mother won't let you.

GOAL: To get to the mall.

ADJUSTMENT /TOOLS: What "adjustments" or "tools" must you perform to achieve your goal?

Mom, you sure look pretty tonight! (To flatter)

Mom, I'll do the dishes every night for a month and take out the garbage and anything else you want me to do. (To bribe)

If you don't let me go, I'll tell everyone how old you are and how much you weigh, and I'll flunk all my classes! (To threaten)

Goals:

1. You want to spend the weekend at a friend's whom your mother does not like.

2. You want to go on your first trip out of town without your parents.

3. You want to date someone your mom and dad does not like.

4. You want to get a job. Your parents want you to study and make good grades.

5. You want to go out at night during the week.

Active verbs:

to ask	to plead
to bribe	to threaten
to punish	to worship
to flatter	to bribe
to warn	to flirt
to tantalize	to avoid
to refuse	to overwhelm
to examine	to beseech
to harm	to request
to admire	to irritate
to tease	to bait
to mock	to badger
to kid	to chastise
to caution	to praise

COACHING TIPS: Did each student in the improvisation pick a set of adjustments and tools? Were they believable?

LESSON THIRTY-NINE

Who Was That Masked Man?

Group Improvisation With Hidden Identities

OBJECTIVE: To think logically, creating moment-to-moment reality while assuming a designated character in a group improvisation.

ACTIVITY: Three to five students engage in an improvisation. One student is the designated moderator of a talk show concerning a specific issue. The other students assume the characters listed below the subject to be discussed. At no time is the moderator to reveal the profession or occupation of the talk show guests. After the improvisation, the class may guess the profession or occupation of each guest based on their participation in the discussion.

1. Subject: Marijuana should be legalized.

>   Panel: A drug addict
>
>   A priest
>
>   A narcotics detective
>
>   A parent of a drug user who died of an overdose
>
>   A social worker

2. Subject: There should be a mandatory eleven-month school year.

>   Panel: A high school drop out
>
>   A single parent
>
>   A tenth grader
>
>   A high school superintendent

3. Subject: The death penalty should be mandatory for anyone covicted of drug dealing.

>   Panel: A death row inmate
>
>   A parent of a convicted drug dealer
>
>   A parent whose son/daughter died of an overdose
>
>   A narcotics detective

4. Subject: There should be no age restrictions to view a film in a motion picture theater.

>   Panel: A Catholic priest
>
>   A fifteen-year-old student
>
>   A film producer

A conservative parent

COACHING TIPS: Students should view the question from the point of view of the character they are playing. After the session, ask the class to identify each of the characters. If one character was not clear, ask the class what were some of the questions or answers that the character could have chosen.

LESSON FORTY
Places, Animals And Inanimate Objects
Three Person Improvisations

OBJECTIVE: To think logically and spontaneously, creating moment-to-moment reality while dealing with elements of conflict in an acting ensemble.

ACTIVITY: Select three students. The trio must take a given place, an animal and an inanimate object and incorporate them in an improvisation. One person must want something (it should be a matter of life and death) from another person who does not want to give it to her. The student who wants something must execute four actions/tasks: to ask, to plead, to bribe and to threaten, in that order. The third student can join with either of the others. They have one minute to confer before beginning.

1. Disneyland, a cobra and a drinking mug

2. Alaska, a tiger and a piano

3. Italy, a dinosaur and a telephone

4. Saudi Arabia, a giant turtle and binoculars

5. Brazilian rain forest, a camel and a knife

6. Bottom of the Pacific Ocean, an anteater and a camera

7. On the moon, a talking parrot and an ax

8. In a spaceship, a kangaroo and a lawn mower

9. India, a penguin and a shovel

10. On top of the Empire State Building, a bulldog and a typewriter

11. Africa, a panda bear and a microwave oven

12. Mars, a dog and a stapler

13. Cape Cod, a Bengal tiger and a powder puff

14. New York City, a bull and a chandelier

15. Japan, a zebra and a camera

16. The North Pole, a donkey and a measuring tape

17. Mexico, an ostrich and a yo-yo

18. The Alps, a rattlesnake and a tennis racket

19. Bermuda, a puppy and a basketball

20. The Egyptian pyramids, a monkey and a computer

COACHING TIPS: Students should be encouraged to think in terms of the senses. It is important that all dialogue be taken seriously since the elements of the improvisation are humorous. This will help develop a sense of comedy as it strengthens concentration and imagination. Did the ensemble work well together and create a believable improvisation?

LESSON FORTY-ONE

Three Distinct Characters

Three Person Improvisations

OBJECTIVE: To sustain a specific character while performing an improvisation.

ACTIVITY: Select three students and have them choose one of the following sets of characters. Allow them one minute to decide on a situation and given circumstances.

1. An animal trainer, a tap dancer and a real estate broker

2. A fashion model, a narcotics detective and a three-year-old child

3. A jockey, a senator and a mad scientist

4. A miser, a terrorist and a florist

5. A Chinese cook, a priest and an Olympic weight lifter

6. A motion picture director, an astronaut and a bartender

7. A lifeguard, a secretary and an ice cream salesman

8. A hot air balloonist, a submarine captain and a Christmas tree salesman

9. A trumpet player, a snow shovel operator and a pizza maker

10. A golf pro, a lion tamer and a convenience store clerk

COACHING TIPS: Did the students relate to one another while sustaining their characters? The instructor can suggest a situation to the first group to get the class started.

LESSON FORTY-TWO
Jump, Jump, Jump
Two Person Jump Improvisations

OBJECTIVE: To explore the use of beats in an improvisation and to think logically and spontaneously, creating moment-to-moment reality while dealing with elements of conflict in an acting duo improvisation.

ACTIVITY: Ask the entire class to go to the front of the room and line up. Then select one student. That student is assigned a place from the list below and must immediately start an improvisation incorporating the location. Once he has begun, he may then select another member of the class to join the improvisation. (The actor literally surprises the other actor he has chosen. That is why it is called a "jump improvisation.") The elements of the improvisation are: Someone wants something (it should be a matter of life and death) from someone else and that someone else will not and does not give it to him. The person or persons wanting must execute four actions/tasks in order: to ask, to plead, to bribe and to threaten.

1. At an amusement park	11. At a mall
2. In the park	12. Outside a movie theatre
3. On a cruise ship	13. On the beach
4. At a party	14. In the desert
5. In a church	15. On top of a mountain
6. Outside a restaurant	16. In a shoe store
7. In school	17. In a pizza restaurant
8. Outside a rock concert	18. In a McDonald's
9. At a swimming pool	19. On a ski mountain
10. At an athletic event	20. In a zoo

Students doing this exercise often pre-plan and feel that they have to come up with an award-winning soap opera. Any pre-planning defeats the purpose of this exercise. Students should use simple tasks, such as trying to borrow someone's skis, trying to borrow money, etc. It is important to keep it simple.

COACHING TIPS: Was the dialogue taken seriously since the elements of the improvisation can be humorous and sometimes ridiculous? This will help develop a sense of comedy as it strengthens concentration and imagination. Did the ensemble work well together and create a believable improvisation?

LESSON FORTY-THREE

What Are We Doing Here?

Group Improvisation

OBJECTIVE: To strengthen the imagination and encourage selectivity.

ACTIVITY: Have a student begin a group improvisation by performing a specific physical activity related to a selected topic from the list below. The instructor then asks other students to join her with other physical activities that are part of the group topic.

EXAMPLE: An operating room. Assign someone as a patient. Add a doctor. Add another doctor. A nurse to assist each doctor. An anesthesiologist. Interns who are watching or assisting the doctor in the operation and so on.

1. An operating room

2. Fortune tellers' convention

3. Go-go dancers

4. Cooks in a large restaurant

5. Senior citizens on tour

6. Boxers at a gym

7. Patrons at a hair salon

8. A caveman acting out the kill to friends

9. A group of soldiers guarding a castle

10. A group of people watching the Wimbledon tennis championship

11. Ballet dancers warming up for a performance

12. Astronauts landing and walking on the moon

13. A group of circus performers

14. A group of rodeo performers

15. A group on an African safari

16. A workshop where shoes are made by hand

17. A group of Santa's helpers making toys

18. Martians examining earthlings on a spaceship

19. A group of various aged individuals at the beach

20. A group warming up for a marathon

COACHING TIP: Did each student clearly create a physical task that depicted the activity of the group? Were they believable as a group?

LESSON FORTY-FOUR

Frozen Bench

Two Person Improvisation

OBJECTIVE: To sustain a character while creating moment-to-moment reality during an improvisation.

ACTIVITY: Two actors are seated on a park bench. One is a meteorologist who predicts it is going to rain for forty nights and forty days. The other person is a:

1. Mary Kay Cosmetics lady

2. mad scientist

3. casting agent from Hollywood

4. creature from outer space

5. priest

6. dentist

7. juvenile delinquent

8. three-year-old child

9. black belt karate champion

10. teenage vampire

COACHING TIPS: Was the characterization specific and believable? Did the students create moment-to-moment reality during the improvisation? Ask the other students to comment on the above two questions, but always direct their answers or comments to you, the instructor, and not the students performing.

LESSON FORTY-FIVE

Zap On A Bench

Two Person Improvisation

OBJECTIVE: To sustain a character while creating moment-to-moment reality during an improvisation.

ACTIVITY: Two chairs are placed side by side representing a bench. Two students are selected to begin the exercise. One student sits on the bench and the other student approaches and sits next to the first student. The first student assumes the character of a gullible teen. The second student is a patient who has escaped from a mental institution. He thinks he is one of the following:

Suggested characters:

1. a wealthy matron
2. a Chinese cook
3. a crippled girl
4. an airline stewardess
5. a meteorologist
6. a veterinarian
7. a librarian
8. an orphan
9. a model
10. an Olympic swimmer

11. a criminal lawyer
12. a sports coach
13. the Queen of England
14. a clergyman
15. a college student
16. a yoga expert
17. a karate expert
18. a magician
19. a ballet dancer
20. a scientist

COACHING TIPS: Were the characterizations specific and believable? Did the students create moment-to-moment reality during the improvisation? Ask the other students to comment on the above questions.

LESSON FORTY-SIX

Solo Entrances

One Person Preparations

OBJECTIVE: To prepare physically and emotionally before a scene.

ACTIVITY: Each student is given a specific circumstance prior to entering the scene. The class should guess what the student is experiencing.

Enter the stage as if you have just...

1. ...finished a twenty-six mile marathon

2. ...sprained an ankle.

3. ...come in from a blizzard.

4. ...discovered you have a dangerously high fever.

5. ...cut your finger badly.

6. ...begun to feel dizzy.

7. ...come in from a day at the beach with a severe sunburn.

8. ...received very sad news.

9. ...lost the big game.

10. ...come back from working all day chopping wood, mowing lawns and digging ditches.

COACHING TIPS: Make sure the student does not just indicate pain. Ask them exactly what kind of pain it is, where and how it hurts. Be specific! Have students create their own circumstances and perform them and have the class guess what they are doing. Was the student believable?

LESSON FORTY-SEVEN

I Want To Be Alone

One Person Improvisation

OBJECTIVE: To sharpen the senses and stimulate the imagination.

ACTIVITY: Each student picks a unique setting and imagines that a strange man/woman hands the student a package wrapped in green paper and says, "Open this when you are alone" and then disappears into the crowd.

The student should incorporate the three following physical activities:

1. To find a place to go to open the box but first make sure no one is following

2. To open the box

3. To suddenly hear someone approaching

Suggested Locations:

1. a cathedral in England	11. a rock concert
2. a restaurant in Tokyo	12. a mall
3. a bus station in Little Rock	13. a supermarket
4. a McDonald's in Moscow	14. a fish market
5. Grand Central Station	15. a school cafeteria
6. a museum in Italy	16. a church
7. the Vatican	17. Disneyland
8. the Great Wall of China	18. on a beach
9. a zoo	19. World Trade Center
10. a school gym	20. a movie theater

COACHING TIPS: Start the exercise with a student who is comfortable with pantomime and use him as a model. Were the three activities clear and distinct? Was the student believeable?

LESSON FORTY-EIGHT

What's Happening?

Two Person Obscure Dialogue Scene

OBJECTIVE: To think creatively, logically and spontaneously, creating moment-to-moment reality while improvising.

ACTIVITY: Select two students. Those students must agree on what the scene is about and what goals they must accomplish. The dialogue cannot be changed or altered. The two students must be specific while executing their physical activities.

Scene 1

A: Hey, come over here.

B: Just a minute, let me finish what I'm doing.

A: You just won't believe it!

B: Okay, I just finished. Here I come.

A: Well, what do you think?

B: Amazing! Just amazing!

A: Who could have done it?

B: I don't know. It's just incredible!

Scene 2

A: We're almost finished.

B: I'm happy about that.

A: Give me that.

B: Here.

A: Thanks. How does that look?

B: Good.

A: Are you glad we did it?

B: I wasn't sure when we started.

A: I wasn't either.

B: It does look good.

A: I know. I couldn't have done it alone. Thanks.

Scene 3

A: Is that the way you want it?

B: I think so. What do you think?

A: It's yours. You can do what you want with it.

B: I know. But I'm a little nervous.

A: Why?

B: It's the first time I've ever owned one.

A: You want to try something else?

B: Okay. Give me a hand.

A: Where do you want it?

B: Let's go over here.

A: Here?

B: Yes.

A: Now what?

B: Let's look at it for a while.

A: You've got to live with it, not me.

B: Yeah, I know.

COACHING TIPS: Were the goals clear? Were the students specific in their execution of physical activities? Have the students observing guess what the students were doing. Was it clear to the students what was taking place? Ask the students what could have been done to make it clearer. With this new information, have the students do the exercise again.

LESSON FORTY-NINE

Say What You Mean!

Solo Intentions

OBJECTIVE: To choose the desired meaning to convey with the text.

ACTIVITY: Each student should be assigned one of the following texts to execute:

1. Repeat the following sentence with the specific meaning/intention directly under the sentence.

   I'm not going to the dance with Bob.

   1. <u>I'M</u> not going with Bob! (Somebody else might want to go to the dance with him but not this girl!)

   2. I'm <u>NOT</u> going to the dance with Bob! (For the hundredth time I tell you, no!)

   3. I'm not going to the dance with <u>BOB</u>. (I'm going to the dance with Fred.)

   4. I'm not going to the <u>DANCE</u> with Bob. (I'm going bowling with him, not to the dance.)

2. Assign students to read one of the following sentences aloud after selecting a specific meaning from the list below.

   A. What can I do for you?
   B. Did you have a good day?
   C. What are you doing here?
   D. Come back and see us again.

1. with fear	6. with pride
2. with suspicion	7. with sorrow
3. with joy	8. with shame
4. with fatigue	9. with enthusiasm
5. with anger	10. with sadness

COACHING TIPS: Was the student specific with her choices? Did she communicate the meaning? Was the student believable?

LESSON FIFTY
Solo Improvisation

OBJECTIVE: To stimulate the imagination and sharpen pantomime skills.

ACTIVITY: Select a student to enter Stage Right, cross to Center Stage and observe one of the following activities:

1. A tennis match	11. A track meet
2. A football game	12. A wrestling match
3. A swimming race	13. A NASCAR race
4. A baseball game	14. A ping-pong game
5. An Olympic ice skater	15. An air balloon race
6. A basketball game	16. A July 4th fireworks display
7. A soccer game	17. A snail race
8. A lacrosse game	18. A horse race
9. A volleyball game	19. A polo match
10. A boxing match	20. An ice hockey game

COACHING TIPS: Was the student specific as he watched? Try to have the student create a set of given circumstances before entering to do the improvisation. Perhaps he can recreate a spectator sporting event he experienced.

DEFINITION OF TERMS

ACTING: Simulated behavoir for the purpose of creating an illusion of reality, a behavoir projected by voice and movement to an audience.

ACTION/TASK: What the actor wants to accomplish in a scene; his inner motivation. The active pursuit of the actor's goal.

ADJUSTMENT/TOOL: Refers to specific, well-chosen phrases. Examples: with sympathy, with understanding, with hostility, with distrust, with disbelief, with hesitation. May also apply to words such as coolly, haughtily, disinterested, etc. Enable the actor to accomplish his "actions." The term "tool" is also used to describe the actor's voice, ability to move, memorize, concentrate and break down scenes. Anything that makes up the "tools" of his/her craft.

ARTICULATION: The clear, distinct and accurate formation and execution of speech sounds.

IMPROVISATION: Scenes that are created and performed spontaneously by actors who make up their own dialogue and actions.

INFLECTION: The rise and fall of the voice from one pitch level to another.

INTENTION: What the actor really feels and thinks, not just the literal meaning of the dialogue; an actor's purpose for being in the scene.

MOMENT-TO-MOMENT REALITY: Instinctive, believable interaction between two actors to whatever takes place at that moment. It is the spontaneous interchange of dialogue and emotion. It should also include physical activity. For example, if a door knob accidentally falls off as an actor enters into a scene, it is not ignored. It is related to and incorporated into the scene.

PANTOMIME: Significant physical activity without words.

PHYSICAL ACTIVITY: The physical movement or business that the actor chooses to do in a scene.

PSYCHOLOGICAL STATE OF MIND: The inner feeling that forces the character to behave.

SIMPLE PHYSICAL ACTION: The process of performing a physical activity and knowing the reason why.

TOOL: See Adjustment

TASK: See Action